CONTENTS

MY PINK STILETTOS - FALL EDITION

2	LIVING OUT LOUD
4	MEET THE AUTHORS SECTION
4	DE'IONA MONAY
6	CAROLYN RICE-SMITH
8	CARMEN A. SMITH
10	IRIS J. CARR
12	TORREE MUNSON
14	DAWN AIRHART WITTE
16	AUTHOR'S SPOTLIGHT - COACH TAYLOR J
18	TAYLOR'S ARTICLE
20	SHAMILA RAMJAWAN
22	WOMEN EMPOWERMENT
25	I SURVIVED BREAST CANCER
26	BEAUTY AND BRAINS

"

When people won't give you an opportunity, Create one!

Larita Rice-Barnes
#IWokeUpToPurpose

LIVING OUT LOUD

You can fulfill your wildest dreams. That's what I'm doing! I've decided to live out loud every day, every second, every minute. You know the old saying you get one life so you might as well live it to the fullest. In a healthy and responsible way that is. My Pink Stilettos was a vision that became a dream come true. A vision to bring women together from all across the world. We all have gifts, skills, talents and abilities. There is a tribe that has been assigned to us all. Your tribe knows your vibe and your vibe attracts your tribe. I want to speak into your life. There's absolutely NOTHING that you can not do. You have divinely been given everything that you need to succeed. It lives on the inside of you. It is called dunamis power. It's supernatural. It enables you to run through troops and leap over walls. It aligns you with greatness and it attracts the people, places and things that will help you get to the next level. Living out loud will cause you to lose some friends. But, guess what the ones that you gain will be the ones that you need. Living out loud will require you to walk away from fear. Fear is a thief and enemy to our destinies. Fear Ain't our friend. It's like Aldi the stock up store. It has all of our blessings stored up. Fear sits in our board rooms and make decisions for us. Fear is that door that we allow to keep us from crossing over to the other side. I want to encourage you today to step out and live loud. No fear. No Excuses Just set your mind and do it. The world is waiting on you to show up and show out.

**Editor In Chief
Dr. Larita Rice-Barnes**

De'Iona Monay

DE'IONA MONAY IS A KEY LEADER OF GILA, INSPIRATIONAL SPEAKER AND PRESIDENT OF XFA FOUNDATION. SHE IS DEDICATED TO BRIDGING THE GAP WITHIN THE EDUCATIONAL SYSTEM BY PROVIDING A PLATFORM FOR FINANCIAL LITERACY COACHING AND SERVICES SUCH AS CREDIT, BUDGETING AND DEBT MANAGEMENT.

Carolyn Rice-Smith

CAROLYN RICE-SMITH IS A WIFE, MOTHER, SISTER AND CONFIDANTE TO MANY. SHE IS A PRAYER WARRIOR AND INTERCESSOR. SHE IS A FAMILY WOMAN. SHE SPEAKS TRUTH TO POWER. SHE IS AN ORDAINED ELDER AND ACTIVE MEMBER OF HER CHURCH EMPOWERMENT OF GRACE. SHE IS A GATEKEEPER OF HER CITY. SHE COMES WITH FIRE IN HER MOUTH AND LOVE IN HEART WITH AN AMPLIFIED MESSAGE COMPELLING PEOPLE TO COME OUT OF BONDAGE! SHE IS THE FOUNDER OF A STEP INTO DESTINY, MAN TO MAN.

Carmen A. Smith

CARMEN A. SMITH IS THE FOUNDER OF NO SUGA COATED WORD MINISTRY, A BLOG DEDICATED TO ENCOURAGING SINGLE MEN AND WOMEN IN THEIR CHRISTIAN WALK. SHE BELIEVES IN LIVING A GOD-FEARING LIFE OF PURPOSE, REGARDLESS OF RELATIONSHIP STATUS. CARMEN CURRENTLY LIVES IN HER NATIVE HOMETOWN OF ST. LOUIS, MO AND SERVES IN MINISTRY AT REDEEMERS HOUSE OF WORSHIP CHRISTIAN CHURCH IN BELLEVILLE, IL.. CARMEN IS THE AUTHOR OF RISING UP TO SOAR: A DEVOTIONAL JOURNAL FOR CHRISTIAN SINGLES PURSUING GOD, SELF-LOVE AND PURPOSE

Iris J. Carr

IRIS J. CARR A NATIVE OF KOSCIUSKO, MISSISSIPPI. SHE IS THE PROUD MOTHER OF TWO BEAUTIFUL DAUGHTERS AND A HANDSOME SON. IRIS IS THE FOUNDER AND CEO OF IMPACT GROWTH ACADEMY, LLC.

Torree Munson

TORREE MUNSON HAS OVERCOME MANY ADVERSITIES, MENTAL AND VERBAL ABUSE, ATTEMPTED SUICIDE, HOMELESSNESS, AND MUCH MORE NOW SHE IS BLAZING A TRAIL FOR THE KINGDOM OF GOD. SHE IS A MOTHER, MINISTER, AUTHOR, LIFE COACH, AND MOTIVATIONAL SPEAKER. AFTER BEING A TWO-TIME DIVORCEE, SHE IS NOW MARRIED TO HER WONDERFUL HUSBAND DR. MUNSON.

Dawn Airhart Witte

DAWN AIRHART WITTE HAS A MISSION: TO INSPIRE OTHERS TO FIND THEIR PURPOSE AND LIVE IT! SHE IS A CERTIFIED LIFE COACH, SPEAKER AND THE FOUNDER OF THE DESIRE TO INSPIRE FOUNDATION, A NON-PROFIT ORGANIZATION THAT WORKS TO BREAK CYCLES OF EXTREME POVERTY. DAWN HAS ALSO PENNED SEVERAL BOOKS, INCLUDING BE... WHICH ENCOURAGES PERSEVERANCE, PURPOSE AND PUTTING KINDNESS OUT INTO THE WORLD.

Coach Taylor J.

COACH TAYLOR J. HAS A PASSION TO HELP OTHERS COMPLETELY TRANSFORM BY ASSISTING WITH GOAL CLARITY, STRATEGIC PLANNING AND UTILIZING WHAT'S ALREADY INSIDE OF THEM. HER GOAL IS TO INSPIRE OTHERS TO LEAVE A LEGACY FOR THEIR BLOODLINES. TAYLOR J. BELIEVES THAT SHE WAS BORN OPTIMISTIC. SHE HAS BEEN FORTIFIED THROUGH EXPERIENCE AND OFFICIALLY CERTIFIED AS A COACH.

Taylor's Article

Go into the deep! At 11 years old I would go swimming with a summer camp that I was apart of. They had a "deep" side that required you to take a test to be able to swim on that side. I didn't know how to swim but many of my friends did, including my brother and all of his friends. I would hang out on the edge of the pool right next to the rope divider and talk to everyone that was on the deep side hoping that nobody would notice that I couldn't swim. One day, someone said to me "Tay come on this side with us!" My heart sunk AND I REPLIED "Oh I need to take my test!" Everyone chimed in and encouraged me to take the test that day but they didn't know that I couldn't swim. In that moment I knew I needed to learn how to swim FAST! As soon as the attention was off of me for a moment, I slipped in the water at the rope divider, went under water and did what I knew how to get to the other side of the pool. My brother signaled for me to catch the life guard that was walking in my direction. I waved the life guard down confidently but I was terrified on the inside! He blew the whistle and signaled for everyone to get out so that I could test for "the deep side". I got in at 7ft and he told me to swim to the other side when I was ready. I decided to not take too much time so I took the deepest breath I could into my lungs, went under AND KICKED AS HARD AS I COULD! I pulled that water back with all of my might! I was determined to pass the test by just making it to the other side! I felt my finger tips touch the pool wall, I came up and looked around to see that everyone was clapping and cheering me on! I PASSED THE DEEP WATER TEST AND GAINED ACCESS TO THE MATURE SIDE! God wants you to step out of your comfort zone and go out into the deep! Thats where your abundance is. What you need to pass the test is already on the inside of you! You have the skillset, the support and an opportunity. Now you Just have to step out on faith and let your net down! When you actually step out on faith, God is going to blow your mind! He did it for Simon, in Luke 5 and he wants to do it for you. Go out into the deep.

Coach Taylor J.

Shamila Ramjawan

SHAMILA FROM SOUTH AFRICA, IS FORMER MRS. JOHANNESBURG 2019. SHE IS A RENOWNED, FORMIDABLE AND WELL-RESPECTED ENTREPRENEUR, LECTURER AT THE UNIVERSITY OF SOUTH AFRICA (UNISA) AND IS A MULTIPLE GLOBAL AWARDEE AND SPEAKER. SHE IS THE FOUNDER OF THE PRINCESSD MENSTRUAL CUP, A 10 YEAR REUSABLE SANITARY PRODUCT AND FOUNDER/TALK SHOW HOST OF THE "RED CORNER CHAT".

WOMEN EMPOWERMENT

HENA PAYGHAM

Shekilla was a young girl who is forced to marry at a very young age.

She has thousands of hopes. She is entering a new phase of life and is not aware of the bad days that are ahead of her.

Shekila, who was just 18 and has two children considered herself the happiest woman on earth with her husband and two sons. She decides to have an angel with her two sons at home. She finally got pregnant and her home filled with joy. But these pleasures did not last long. Shekila's husband was killed by his enemy before he can see his little angel. And this was when Shekila's troubles began!

She gives birth to her daughter with many problems that came her way. She did not only become a mother but, also a woman who is forced into the role of a father and a mother for her children! Shekila had no choice but to return to her parents' home again. This was exactly during the time that the Taliban ruled in Afghanistan.

There were many constraints to women's advancement. Constraints were to the extent that women did not have the freedom to go out of the house.

Shekila did not accept defeat. She would leave home wearing the burka. She seemingly faced thousands of challenges while going to school to further her education

According to Shekila, when she was sitting in class, her mind stopped being activated. She couldn't even write whenever she thought of her children! Being a mom for her was so difficult during this time. **When Shekilla would be sitting in class there wasn't a moment that went by she didn't have her children on her mind. She wondered what her little children were eating? What are they doing? Those thoughts persisted for a long time. She did not accept defeat and never gave up. On the contrary, she was getting stronger every day.**

Finally, despite all the difficulties Shekila successfully completed her education and became a journalist at Kabul University. She also worked in a kindergarten class while completing her education. She wanted to meet the needs of her children.

Shekila says "I only had one goal and that was to work hard to challenge myself. I didn't want my children to feel anything. I didn't want them to work on the streets like other kids or feel like orphans. After graduating from the university, Shekila started working at Tolo TV, the largest media platform in Afghanistan. graduation **everything changes. Her life takes on a different color.** Shekila no longer considers herself a lonely, helpless woman but rather, one of the most successful journalists of that time.

Not only did she become a successful mother but she also became the voice of other women.

Shekila became very famous and earned the title of bravest female journalist. She worked very hard not just for her children but for her country and her people.

During this time a woman named Ms. Ibrahim Khail, reported on issues that attracted public attention.

She was personally investigating corrupt and bribery disputes by members of the government. She extensively investigated inhumane acts against women.

She produced a documentary about a 15-year-old girl who had been raped. With the release of this documentary, the international community became shocked and outraged. To the extent that former President Hamid Karzai visits the girl and orders that her case be investigated in court **faster.** Shekila's documentary and critical films are so unique that she has been selected as the journalist of the year many times and has received national and international awards. Once in a while **Shekila's life still takes a different color again.**

On January 21, 2016 a cruel and horrific attack on Tolo TV takes place and everything changes. On this day Shekila **goes to the office and there was a brutal attack.** Hours had elapsed since the accident, but no news came from Shekila. Her children calls her many times but her phone **was switched off.** One of their neighbors comes and tells her daughter that your mother died Your mother is no longer with us. Her children is frustrated and they don't know what to do. They were crying and shocked. They left without wearing shoes looking for their mother to no avail. In despair, they head back home. When they arrived a miracle happened. Their mother opens the door for them! It was unbelievable for her children that their mother survived the accident. They hugged their mother and wept for joy! It had been a dark day in the life of Shekila and her children. All of Shekila's colleagues had died. After **seeing how this had affected her children,** Shekila didn't want to put her children through this again. For the sake of her children, she abandoned all of her fame and accomplishments and went to one of the countries in Europe. Today her children are safe. Finally, her children have everything that they want. The hardships of their super mother has made them successful.

Hena Paygham.

Dr. Missy Johnson

I SURVIVED BREAST CANCER

Dr. Missy was a rising star in an Americas Fortune 100 company. Suddenly her life changed, and she lost everything. Dr. Missy turned her tragedies into triumphs to create transformation for herself and others. She's the CEO of Fearless Women Rock LLC, a faith-based platform for women to share their stories.

After a near-death experience, six months later, I was diagnosed with Breast Cancer Stage 3. My body levels to fight cancer was weak. It felt like my body and mind was shutting down. No doctors, nurses, or preachers could tell me anything.

One day I prayed and asked God for his will to be done. I told God I don't have the strength mentally to take another setback to my body and mind. I said, Lord, I need you to fight on my behalf because I just don't have it anymore. I leaned on my Faith. God reminded me how he brought me out of a three percent chance of living six months earlier, so just trust the process. I am a survivor of cancer because of my Faith in God and trust beyond my own understanding. When God gives you one more day, make it matter. Your story matters, and your voice is valuable so keep moving.

For speaking opportunities CONTACT:

Fearlesswomenrockllc@gmail.com
or
AskDrMissy on all social media platforms.

Beauty and Brains

CANESHA HENRY (CJH BRAND)

If you're natural and in this case meaning no relaxers, you've probably become a researcher, scientist, stylist and chemist by now! We are in the age of influencers, and vloggers and there's content being created everywhere to tell you everything you should be doing with your hair. You've probably read you should only use sulfate-free shampoo, and let me just tell you why this is a BIG no in my salon. Sulfate is a cleansing agent that is used to deeply clarify the scalp and de-clog cuticles. Sure, after shampooing your hair it'll feel a more dry, but that's because you've stripped your hair of build up and debris, and to add natural oils and vitamins in your hair you should always follow up with a conditioner. Your shampoo and conditioning process is way more important than any other product you can buy. This is often times what many are less likely to invest in. Making this investment can help prevent excessive shedding, breakage and dryness. Sulfate-free shampoo should not be your main shampoo.

BONUS TIP: Shampoo with warm water and rinse your conditioner with cool water

BIO – In 4 short years she has worked on plays and movie sets, with your favorite artists and TV and radio personalities. She helps to cultivate and monetize skills by way of coaching and counseling. She's known for her creative ideas, faith and wisdom. CJ passionately works to improve brands professionally and personally to attract the money you want to make.

INFO@CJHBRAND.COM

WWW.CJHBRAND.COM

 CJHBRAND

 CJHBRAND

Made in United States
Orlando, FL
13 November 2023